FRONT COVER: Artistic rendering of Ged Brockie playing a Hofner Senator guitar

Fastlines: The Combined Cassette and Booklet Tutor

Cassette (mp3s) and Documentation

Copyright 2016 GMI - Guitar & Music Institute

ISBN 978-0-9955088-5-9

Music composed and recorded by Ged Brockie

Gary Fimister - Bass and Dave Stewart - Drums

Recording and mixdown at K.S.M. Recording Studios- Edinburgh

Music typeset by G.B. Guitar & Music Institute

Graphic Design by Chris Donaldson

Proof reading by Douglas Urquhart

TABLE OF CONTENTS

FOREWORD FROM GED BROCKIE

Thank you for purchasing Fastlines Intermediate Jazz Method, a work that first saw the light of day back in the early 1990's and through digital technology has now been re designed and re published for a new generation of guitarists. This is the second of three jazz tutors in the Fastlines range which in total consists of nine books

I have had the joy of performing, teaching and studying the guitar throughout my life. I feel, now more than ever, the pursuit of expression through music and the arts in general can be a transformational experience and a much needed counterweight to the immediacy of the Internet world we now live in.

I created Fastlines so that people could work from a collection of musical ideas that they could use in improvised solo situations. Coming up with lines that make musical sense is one of the great challenges when improvising and that is how the Fastlines concept was born. As well as this, I wanted to provide an understanding of how each line functioned. Through this understanding, lines could be altered and changed to fit various harmonic scenarios. The short solo that is included in this book offers the student insight into ways in which different lines can be joined together to create a meaningful improvisation. Backing tracks give context for each of the memorised lines to be realised and heard against and finally, the projects allow for long term development of the lines presented here.

I hope you enjoy using this work and that you will consider the other books in the series which were developed over a two year period. I am confident that they will bring you a deeper understanding of the jazz genre and help you meet your improvisational goals.

Ged Brockie

Ged Brockie has performed in almost every conceivable musical scenario over a thirty year period. His own band recordings comprise his own compositions, arrangements and performance with some of Scotland's finest musicians (The Mirror's Image - Circular Records 2009, The Last View From Mary's Place - Circular Records 2004). He was one of the main writers in the Scottish Guitar Quartet (SGQ) recording three albums (Near The Circle 2001, Fait Accompli 2003, Landmarks 2005) touring across Europe to critical acclaim. The DVD "Five Innovations For Guitar & Orchestra - Circular Records 2011" featured Ged with a twenty one piece orchestra. He has also worked with the RSNO, OSO, Carl Davis, Hummie Mann, West End shows on tour, TV & radio, music industry events, all levels of music education from high school to university and has a wide range of compositions used in film, TV and media.

Ged is the lead instructor and driving force behind GMI and guides the programs of learning within it.

www.gedbrockie.com

FASTLINES

FASTLINES Jazz Intermediate/Advanced by Ged Brockie

FASTLINE 1

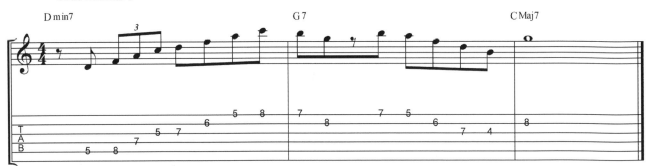

FASTLINE One
Tempo: 168

Scale used: C major.

Tech./harmonic aspects: Pull-offs, stretch fingerings, D minor seventh and G dominant seventh arpeggios.

Comments:

1. Increase your level of attack with the pick as you ascend the Dmin7 arpeggio.

2. Although this Fastline is fingered for position five, it can easily be played in a variety of positions on the neck.

FASTLINE 2

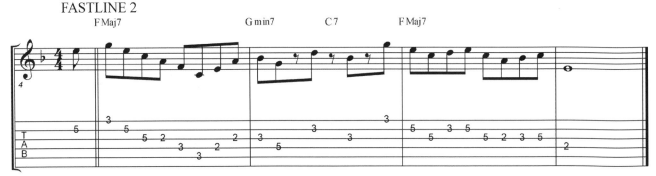

FASTLINE Two
Tempo: 200

Scale used: F major.

Tech./harmonic aspects: Major 4th intervals, syncopated rhythms, sequential patterns, G & A minor seventh arpeggios, F major seventh arpeggio.

Comments:

1. The substitution of chord III (Amin7 arpeggio) for chord I (F major) is quite common.

2. Bar two could cause you a problem with having to play off the beat.

3. Accent the first and fifth notes of bar three.

FASTLINE 3

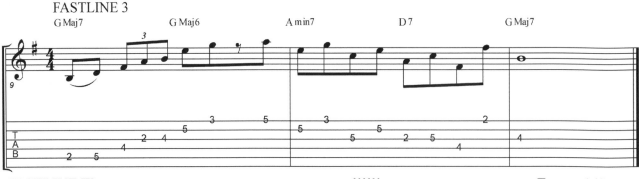

FASTLINE Three
Tempo: 160

Scales used: G major.

Tech./harmonic aspects: Hammer-ons, B minor seventh arpeggio, descending sequence in thirds.

Comments:

1. Again, chord III (B minor) is substituted for chord I (G major). The second bar is best played with a rolling finger technique in the left hand.

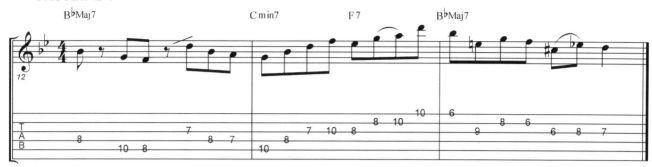

FASTLINE Four
Tempo: 176

Scale used: B flat major.

Tech./harmonic aspects: Slides, hammer-ons, G minor & E flat major seven sharp eleven arpeggios.

Comments:

1. Bar two contains both the Gmin7 and E flat Maj7 sharp 11 arpeggios. The F & D notes in bar two are approached by neighbourtones and chromatic approach tones.

FASTLINE 5

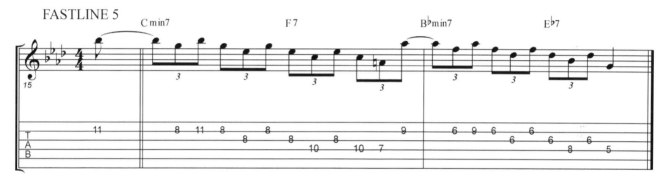

FASTLINE Five
Tempo: 144

Scale used: B flat major/A flat major.

Tech./harmonic aspects: Triplet rhythm used over the entire line.

Comments:

1. Although four chords are notated, the two minor chords are emphasized more by thier respective arpeggios than the dominant seventh chords.

FASTLINE 6

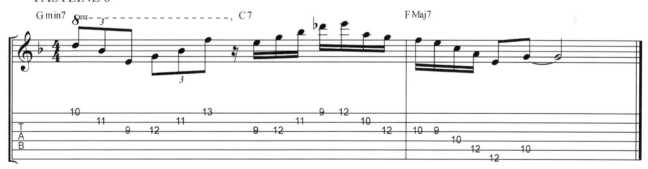

FASTLINE Six
Tempo: 116

Scale used: F major.

Tech./harmonic aspects: D flat diminished arpeggio and use of triplet and sixteenth rhythms.

Comments:

1. The first two beats are played up one octave.

2. D flat diminished substituted over the C7 chord. *Rule: A dominant chord can be substituted by a diminished chord one semi-tone higher.*

FASTLINE 7

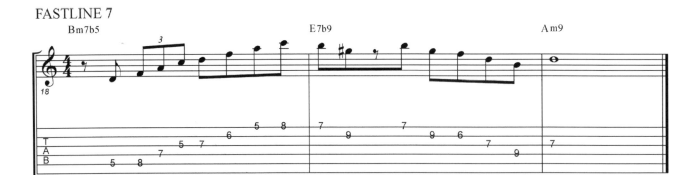

FASTLINE Seven
Tempo: 160

Scale used: A harmonic minor.

Tech./harmonic aspects: Stretch-fingerings, A harmonic minor used throughout.

Comments:

1. D minor seven is substituted for B minor seven flat five chord in bar one.

2. In bar two, F diminished is substituted for E7 flat nine.

FASTLINE 8

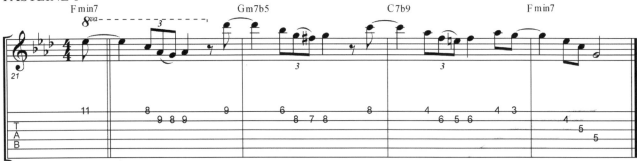

FASTLINE Eight
Tempo: 200

Scale used: F minor (natural).

Tech./harmonic aspects: Pull-offs, stretch fingerings, repeated descending rhythmic patterns.

Comments:

1. The second two notes in each of the triplets should be execeuted as pull-offs.

FASTLINE 9

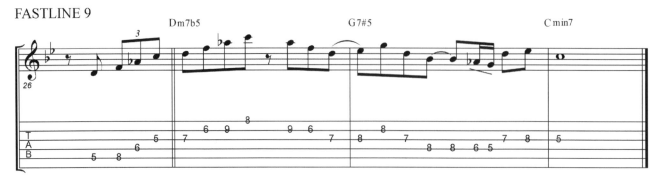

FASTLINE Nine
Tempo: 138

Scales used: C minor (natural).

Tech./harmonic aspects: Stretch-fingerings, hammer-ons, slides.

Comments:

1. Take special care with left hand fingerings throughout this line.

2. The B flat notes in bar two can be replaced with B natural. The scale now being played would be C harmonic.

FASTLINE 10

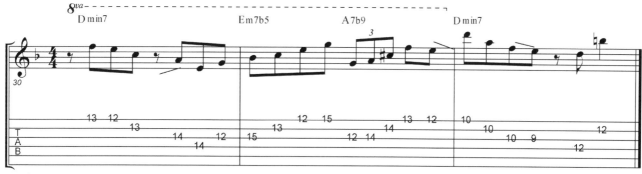

FASTLINE Ten   Tempo: 160

Scale used: D natural/harmonic minor.

Tech./harmonic aspects: Slides. The B natural note in the last bar produces a major sixth interval from the D root. The note comes from the melodic minor scale of D.

Comments:

1. As the whole lick can be played above the twelfth fret, it may be desirable to practice the whole Fastline down one octave to begin with.

FASTLINE 11

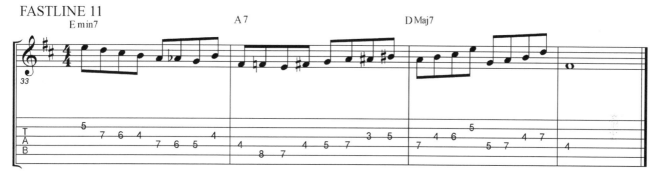

FASTLINE Eleven   Tempo: 246

Scales used: D major/B flat diminished.

Tech./harmonic aspects: Stretch scales, chromatic approach tones, sequential patterns.

Comments:

1. The B flat diminished scale starts proper on the second beat of bar two. This scale uses the same substitution rules as the diminished arpeggios played over dominant seventh chords.

FASTLINE 12

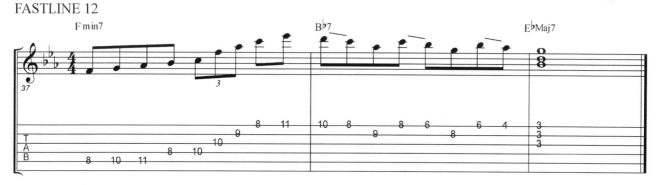

FASTLINE Twelve   Tempo: 152

Scale used: E flat major.

Tech./harmonic aspects: Slides, sequential patterns, F minor arpeggio.

Comments:

1. This Fastline is very diatonic in regards to the under-pinning harmony and would be suitable in a number of musical styles.

FASTLINE 13

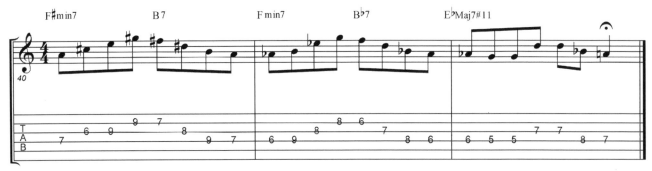

FASTLINE Thirteen   Tempo: 240
Scale used: E major, E flat major/lydian.
Tech./harmonic aspects: Major and dominant seventh arpeggios. Repeated melodic pattern played chromatically through the changes.
Comments:
1. Fastline thirteen makes use of major seventh arpeggios played over related minors. For example, "A" major seventh is played over F sharp minor seventh giving an F sharp minor ninth sound.
2. The last note played in bar three is commonly called the sharpened eleventh tone. If you like this sound and want to incorporate it into your playing, simply count up to the fourth note in a major scale and raise it be one semi-tone (one fret).

FASTLINE 14

FASTLINE Fourteen   Tempo: 240
Scale used: C minor (harmonic).
Tech./harmonic aspects: Scalar run, stretch notes.
Comments:
1. This is a classic minor line that emphasises just how flexible the harmonic minor scale can be. Note how the line ends on the ninth tone of the C minor ninth chord.

FASTLINE 15

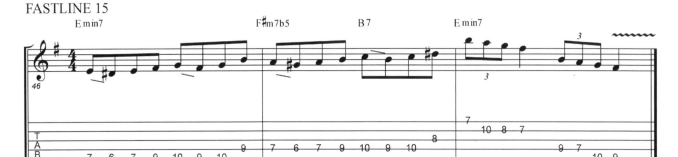

FASTLINE Fifteen   Tempo: 168
Scale used: E minor (harmonic).
Tech./harmonic aspects: Slides, sequential patterns, repeated figures, vibrato.
Comments:
1. The hardest part of this line is to execute the slides in bar one and two smoothly. Practice first with a metronome.

FASTLINE 16

FASTLINE Sixteen   Tempo: 248

Scale used:G minor (harmonic).

Tech./harmonic aspects: Chromatic approach tones, three over two rhythms, stretch-fingerings, neighbour tones.

Comments:

1. Bar two (beats three and four) and bar three are where the most care is needed. The F sharp to D and E flat to C sharp should be played with fingers three to four and one to three respectively.

2. Listening carefully to the mp3 should clear up any difficulties with the timing needed to play bar three.

FASTLINE 17

FASTLINE Seventeen   Tempo: 116

Scale used: C major.

Tech./harmonic aspects: Slides, chromatic approach tones.

Comments:

1. A string skip is needed to jump from the G to D note at the end of beat one. Try playing with hammer-ons/pull-offs as well as alternate picking.

FASTLINE 18

FASTLINE Eighteen   Tempo: 192

Scale used: A major.

Tech./harmonic aspects: Stretch-fingerings.

Comments:

1. This is a simple diatonic major idea that would be good for an ending. Try playing it down the octave as well.

FASTLINE 19

FASTLINE Nineteen   Tempo: 260

Scales used: F major.

Tech./harmonic aspects: Chromatic approach tones, stretch-fingerings, slides.

Comments:

1. Sounds best when played fast. Fastline nineteen works just as well over B flat major and D minor chords.

2. Take care with fingerings in bar two (beat two) and the stretch slide from the B flat to the A natural note at the end of bar three.

FASTLINE 20

FASTLINE Twenty   Tempo: 138

Scales used: A minor (harmonic).

Tech./harmonic aspects: Stretch fingering, chromatic approach and target tones.

Comments:

1. Although this line may look complex, by seeing it as a physical pattern on the fret-board makes for easier memorisation. In regards to the theory behind this line, you could view it as a basic F major triad (notes three, seven and eleven) targeted by a descending chromatic line.

FASTLINES SOLO

FASTLINE Solo

The Fastline solo contains most, if not all, of the techniques outlined in the line by line section. Several Fastlines have been lifted directly out of the Fastline lick section and placed in the solo, and new ideas have also been added. For more details of the Fastline solo, and how to get the best out of it, turn to the projects section found later in this booklet.

Intro: Scalar intro which includes a finger stretch.
Bars 2-3: II-V in B flat major. Part of Fastline number five in bar three.
Bars 4: Use of B diminished line over the B dominant seven chord (includes finger stretches).
Bars 5-6: Down-step modulation is used in these two bars (IMaj-Imin). The scales used are E flat major (Ionian mode) in bar five and D flat major in bar six (Dorian).
Bars 7-8-9: II-V-I in the key of C minor. Based loosly upon Fastline fourteen. Note that the C minor chord is pivotal in linking between the keys of C minor (chord I) and B flat major (chord II)
Bars 9-10-11-12: Use of string skipping in bar then. Chromatic approach tones used in bar eleven which are repeated in bar twelve.
Note: To play along with the backing chords to the solo, simply pan speakers left or right. Tempo 168 bpm

BACKING TRACKS

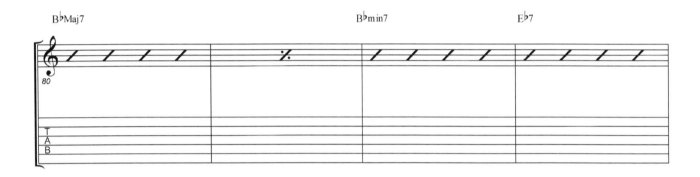

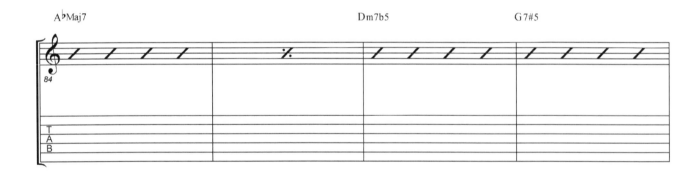

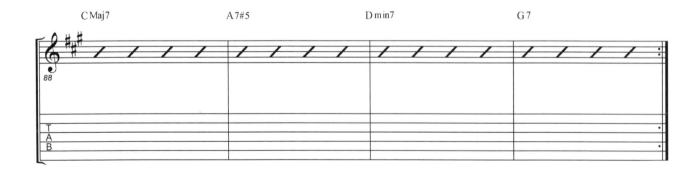

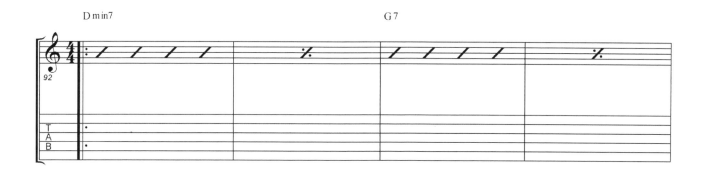

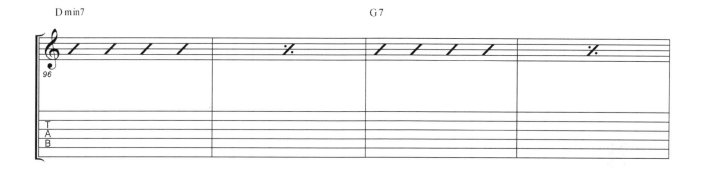

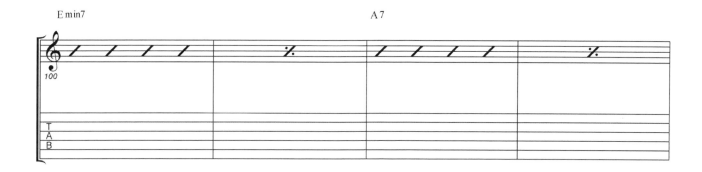

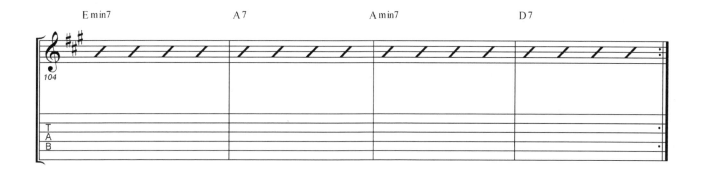

G min7

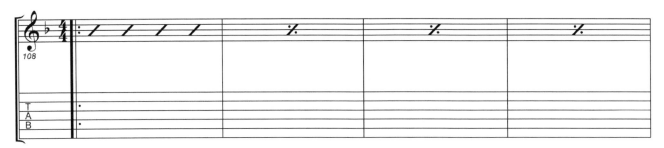

G min7

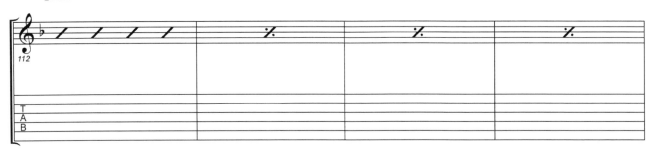

A♭min7

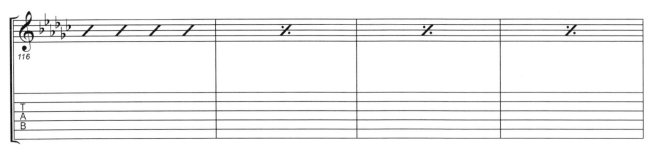

G min7

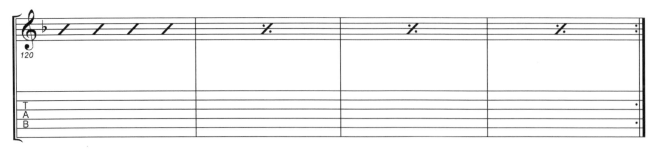

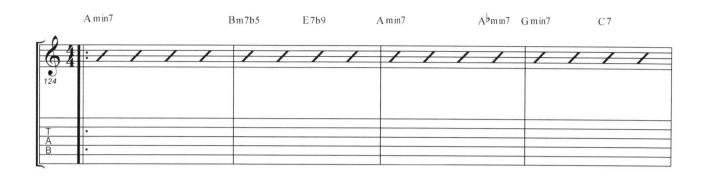

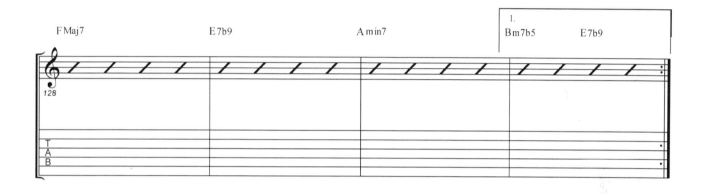

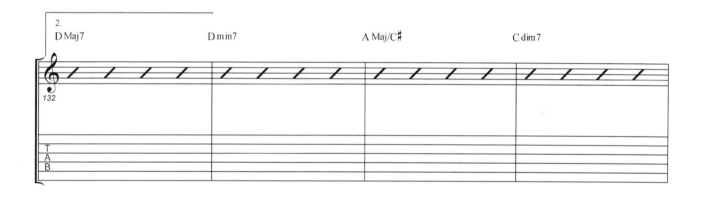

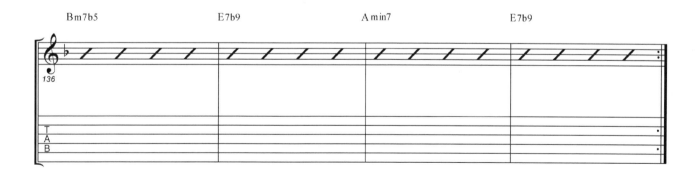

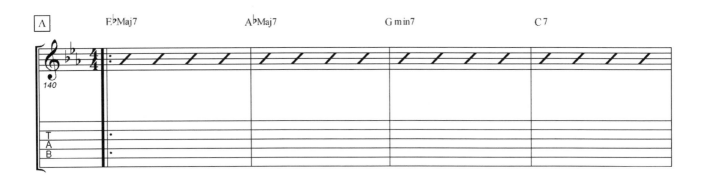

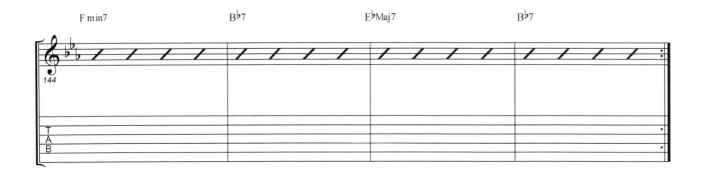

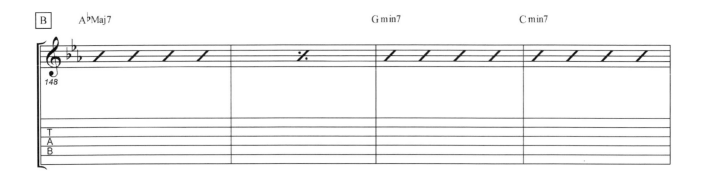

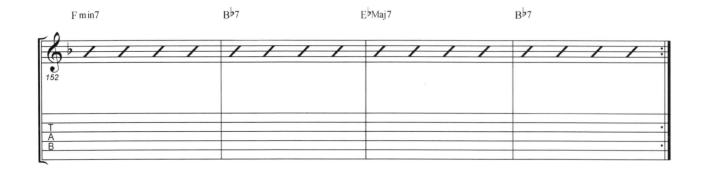

FASTLINE PROJECTS

FASTLINES JAZZ INT./ADV. PROJECTS

Substitution

Learning to use one arpeggio over various chord types is an excellent way of producing new and exciting sounds. Fastlines one, two and four all contain substitute arpeggios.

In Fastline one (bar two) for example, a Bmin7 flat five arpeggio is substituted for the G7 chord, giving us a G9 sound. Fastline two uses the III chord of F major (Amin7) in bar one and Fastline four includes a Gmin7 arpeggio playing over a Cmin7 chord.

Write out the Diatonic chord progressions of several major keys and play the resulting chords in arpeggio form. Take one chord from the chosen key, record it for five or so minutes then experiment playing the other arpeggios over it. You will find some surprising sounds. Chord III over chord I works well, as does VI for I and II for VII and V.

Neighbour Tones

Upper and lower neighbour tones are used by Jazz musicians to decorate scales and arpeggios.

A neighbour tone is a note that is a tone above, or a semi-tone below, the target note. Fastline four (bar three) and Fastline fifteen are good examples of this.

Neighbour tones help to extend small scale fragments or arpeggios into usable lines, as well as being excellent as warm-up exercises. Apply this concept to all the scales and arpeggios you currently work with, using the above examples as your guide.

Wide Interval Playing

Wide intervals of the fourth, fifth or sixth variety will give your improvisations a new dimension that is not available through constant scalar passages. However, to play this you will need to pick across adjacent strings. Although this idea is dealt with in greater detail in subsequent Fastlines tutors, a start can be made here.

Fastline three may prove difficult to master. If you do encounter difficulty with this line, use a metronome until you can play it smoothly. Use as many different fingerings and positions on the neck as possible.

Triplet Rhythms

If counting and playing three over one is not one of your strong points, then playing Fastline five will have caused problems.

This project will help you develop your rhythmic ideas: write out each Fastline, converting all the rhythms to triplets. Using the metronome is once again essential if long term progress is to be made.

Obviously experimenting with rhythms need not stop with the triplet. Five, six and seven notes per beat are all worth further investigation.

From Major to Minor

This project will enable you to nearly double the amount of Fastlines that you have received in this package in relation to major/minor II-V-I progressions.

Compare Fastlines one and seven. With the exception of one note, G, both lines are almost identical. The line however is played over different chords. Take all the major II-V-I Fastlines and move the harmony down a minor third (three frets). For example, Fastline two would read Dmin7-Emin7 flat five-A7-Dmin7 instead of the current chord symbols. With the minor II-V-I progressions, move the harmony up a minor third (three frets). Fastline ten would now read FMaj-Gmin7-C7-Fmaj7. Some alterations of the melody may be necessary but, for the most part, the lines will sound fine.

Repeated Rhythmic Figures

Fastline eight shows just how effective rhythmic repetition can be in constructing lines, or even complete solos, through chord changes. Repeating a rhythmic phrase like this will give your lines a unified feel. There are plenty of examples in this tutor that can be picked out and applied to other Fastlines, or your own lick ideas. Listen to some of your favourite jazz guitarists and see how much they draw on this technique.

Chromatic Approach Tones

You may have noticed that some of the Fastlines contain sections where the notes move by semitones. Fastlines sixteen, seventeen and twenty are good examples of this. These lines make use of chromatic approach tones. If you do not use them already, then you are missing out on a dynamic improvising tool. All fundamental tones of a chord (rt, 3rd, 5th for example) can be approached by four chromatic tones from above or below. Therefore, if the target tone was a G note, you could approach it from the notes B, B flat, A, A flat or D sharp, E, F, F sharp. Study lines sixteen, seventeen and twenty to get a better understanding of this device before applying it to your own licks.

Fastlines Solo

The Fastlines solo shows how lines can be linked together to produce complete solos. To achieve this, several of the Fastlines used had to be transposed to harmonise with the key centre of B flat major. As well as using existing material, several other lines were introduced to act as links. One last point, bars seven to eight draw from the material in Fastline fourteen but note the different starting point for the idea which changes the sound. This emphasises how Jazz music is an evolving art form. Try constructing your own solos from the remaining Fastlines in this package, interspersing them with your own lines.

Syncopated Rhythms

Bars five and nine in the Fastlines solo are examples of syncopated rhythm. Notes played on the weak part of the beat give a rhythmic contrast to the strong pulse set down by the rhythm section. In both instances, a simple arpeggio has been used (E flat Major seven and C minor seven) but interest has been maintained by the use of syncopation. At first you may find yourself straying onto the strong part of the beat. The best way to rectify this is to use the metronome.

The variations available will only be limited by your imagination - so persevere. Once again, use arpeggios and scales as your source material.

Over The Bar Line

Playing over a constantly changing harmonic background is one of the many challenges facing the jazz guitarist. Making use of common tones however, is one way of easing into new chords and producing continuity in your key changes. Look at the Fastlines solo on page twenty-one. Notice how many times a note is tied over the bar line. This happens even when the chords change Try to ensure that the note tied over is a strong tone in both chords - thirds, fifths and flattened sevenths are good. Take this idea into account when joining several Fastlines together, or when working with your own lines.

QR CODES & LINES

QR CODES

QR CODES FOR VIDEO ON YOUR PHONE OR TABLET!

FASTLINES intro and tuning up notes

The above image is a QR code. These have been provided so you don't need to turn on a computer and quickly hear the relevant audio on your mobile phone or tablet whilst at your music stand.

1. Download a QR code reader from Google Play or the Mac store. There are many free programs.

2. Once downloaded, open up the app and point at the QR code. The relevant mp3 will open for you to play.

3. We tried to embed QR codes beside each musical example, however, there were issues regarding the small size of the QR code as well as spacing and the relevant mp3 file being activated. These pages provide a list for you to refer to and use when studying a specific line, the solo or Backtracks.

QR code for Fastline 1 Jazz Intermediate

QR code for Fastline 2 Jazz Intermediate

QR code for Fastline 3 Jazz Intermediate

QR code for Fastline 4 Jazz Intermediate

QR CODES Cont...

QR code for Fastline 5 Jazz Intermediate

QR code for Fastline 6 Jazz Intermediate

QR code for Fastline 7 Jazz Intermediate

QR code for Fastline 8 Jazz Intermediate

QR code for Fastline 9 Jazz Intermediate

QR code for Fastline 10 Jazz Intermediate

QR code for Fastline 11 Jazz Intermediate

QR CODES Cont...

QR code for Fastline 12 Jazz Intermediate

QR code for Fastline 13 Jazz Intermediate

QR code for Fastline 14 Jazz Intermediate

QR code for Fastline 15 Jazz Intermediate

QR code for Fastline 16 Jazz Intermediate

QR code for Fastline 17 Jazz Intermediate

QR code for Fastline 18 Jazz Intermediate

QR CODES Cont...

QR code for Fastline 19 Jazz Intermediate

QR code for Fastline 20 Jazz Intermediate

QR code for Fastline Jazz Intermediate solo

QR code for Jazz Intermediate Backtrack 1

QR code for Jazz Intermediate Backtrack 2

QR code for Jazz Intermediate Backtrack 3

QR code for Jazz Intermediate Backtrack 4

QR code for Jazz Intermediate Backtrack 5

HAVE YOU DOWNLOADED YOUR AUDIO FILES YET?

1. Book owners should access mp3 files for this book at the following URL...This is NOT a necessary step if you just wish to use the QR codes provided in this book.

   http://www.guitarandmusicinstitute/audiojazzint/

2. For security purposes and in an effort to try and keep piracy to a bearable level you will be asked three questions which relate to words found on pages within this book. You will also be asked for your name and email.

3. A compressed file containing all the mp3 files will be downloadable from a link contained within an email that will be sent to the email address you have stipulated on correct completion of the questions.

4. Make sure to check your spam folder regarding this email just incase nothing turn up within five to ten minutes.

5. Thank you for purchasing this book and supporting further publications from GMI, we really do appreciate it.

PLEASE REVIEW AND STAR RATE THIS BOOK

If you have found this book helpful in your guitar playing development, please take the time to give a review and give the book a star rating. We value your contribution and it helps us when creating more resources for guitarists around the world.

Thanks for your time. Please visit us at the following URL address:

http://www.guitarandmusicinstitute.com

17427216R00020

Printed in Great Britain
by Amazon